CONTENTS

I0409489

"IT IS BOTH GOOD LAW AND GOOD SENSE THAT A MAN WHO IS ATTACKED MAY DEFEND HIMSELF. IT IS BOTH GOOD LAW AND GOOD SENSE THAT HE MAY DO, BUT ONLY DO, WHAT IS REASONABLY NECESSARY."

Palmer v R, [1971] AC 814

SELF-DEFENCE

INTRODUCTION

Self-defence is a crucial concept in the legal world, balancing personal safety with legal responsibility. For someone to successfully claim self-defence, they must meet certain strict conditions that make their actions justifiable in the eyes of the law. This little book explores the various aspects of self-defence, looking at the key elements that form its foundation.

At the core of this concept are four essential requirements that act as a guide for an individual's claim to self-defence: facing a threat of unjustified harm, protecting a valued interest, having a strong belief in the need for defensive action, and using a reasonable amount of force considering the situation.

These basic conditions shape the idea of self-defence, providing a framework for a legal argument to be made.

As this book navigates' through the complexities of self-defence, two important questions arise: Could the person defending themselves have safely walked away, and how immediate was the danger they faced? These questions highlight the intricacies of self-defence, considering the possibility of retreat and the urgency of the perceived threat.

The examination of self-defence goes beyond these basics, looking at factors like the characteristics of the person defending themselves and the mental aspects influencing their reactions. The concept of using excessive force in self-defence is also explored, pushing the boundaries of what is considered reasonable.

Additionally, the legal framework is shaped by the Criminal Law Act 1967 s.3 and the Criminal Justice and Immigration Act 2008 s.76, laws that have influenced and redefined discussions around self-defence. Delving into this exploration, we unravel the complex web of self-defence, revealing the interplay of elements, questions, and legal provisions that form a legal doctrine balancing personal protection with the principles of justice and proportionality.

ASPECTS OF SELF-DEFENCE

Several conditions must be present for an individual to be justified in engaging in self-defence. These can be outlined as follows:

- A threat of unjustified harm;
- A protected interest;
- An honest conviction that defensive action was imperative;
- The use of defensive force deemed reasonable given the circumstances.

In determining whether these elements are satisfied two additional questions may also be asked:

- Was there an opportunity for the defender to withdraw?
- How imminent was the impending attack?

THREAT OF UNJUSTIFIED HARM

In criminal law, the idea of a "threat of unjustified harm" means that someone is facing real and immediate danger or harm without legal justification. This danger could be physical harm, injury, or a threat to their well-being. For an act of self-defence to be considered justified, the person must genuinely believe that they are in immediate danger of harm that is not legally allowed.

Essentially, the threat of unjustified harm requires that the perceived danger is real, not just a possibility. It's important that the person's belief in imminent harm is both sincere and reasonable given the circumstances. If someone reasonably believes they are in danger, the law might permit them to defend themselves. However, if the threat isn't genuine or the response is too much, the claim of self-defence may not be valid.

Overall, the concept of a "threat of unjustified harm" in criminal law aims to balance protecting individuals from harm while ensuring that self-defence claims are based on real fears of immediate danger.

In cases involving the police, the same principles of self-defence and assessing the legitimacy of a threat apply, but there may be specific considerations.

Police officers have the authority to use force when needed to carry out their duties and protect the public. However, the force they use must be reasonable and proportionate to the threat they're dealing with. Whether the concept of a "threat of unjustified harm" applies to the police depends on the specific circumstances of each case. Law enforcement's use of force is typically guided by legal standards and regulations. Investigations into the use of force by police focus on whether the threat was real and if the level of force used was reasonable for the situation.

The idea of the "threat of unjustified harm" isn't just about self-defence but also includes defending innocent third parties in criminal law. If someone believes that an innocent person is in immediate danger of unjustified harm, they may be allowed to intervene to protect that third party. Similar to self-defence, the person intervening must genuinely believe the threat is real, and their response, whether using force or taking other actions, should be reasonable and proportionate to the perceived danger.

The principles of reasonableness and proportionality play a key role in assessing whether the defender's actions were justified.

When it comes to protecting someone else, it gets more legally complex because we need to understand not only the threat but also the defender's reasons and intentions. Laws about defending innocent third parties can differ between places, so the details might vary. In the end, the idea of the "threat of unjustified harm" includes situations where someone takes action to protect not just themselves but also others who are in immediate danger.

PROTECTED INTERESTS

"Protected interests" in common law refer to the rights, values, or entitlements that individuals have, and the legal system works to protect these. These include personal well-being, property, and fundamental rights recognised by the law. Protected interests are crucial for deciding if actions are legal, assessing responsibilities, and ensuring justice in the legal system.

In self-defence, protected interests mean that individuals have the right to defend themselves, their property, or others' well-being from immediate harm. The law acknowledges that people have a valid interest in keeping themselves safe. So, actions taken in self-defence to protect these interests can be considered lawful under certain conditions.

It's important to know that the details of protected interests can vary depending on the jurisdiction and specific laws in place. The concepts of reasonableness, proportionality, and the immediate threat of harm often come into play when deciding if actions taken in self-defence are legal.

The European Convention on Human Rights (ECHR) talks about the right to defend oneself in the context of human rights. According to Article 2 of the ECHR, everyone has the right to life and can use force when necessary to protect themselves or others from immediate and unlawful violence.

The ECHR allows using lethal force in self-defence only when it's absolutely necessary to counter an immediate and serious threat to life. The response must be proportionate, meaning it should match the danger faced to avoid excessive force.

The ECHR also emphasises that state authorities, like law enforcement, must follow these principles. They should use force only when absolutely needed and within the limits of the law. Going beyond what's reasonably required to handle a threat is considered a violation of human rights under the ECHR.

The ECHR's rules on self-defence aim to balance protecting individual rights with the state's duty to maintain public safety and order. How these principles are interpreted and applied can differ among member states and may be influenced by case law and legal developments.

AN HONEST CONVICTION THAT DEFENSIVE ACTION WAS IMPERATIVE

The necessity for defensive action means that any actions taken in self-defence must be absolutely needed to protect yourself or others from immediate harm. In legal terms, it emphasises that using force or defensive measures is only okay when there's no other reasonable choice to avoid the danger. When claiming self-defence, you have to show that your response was necessary to counteract a real and immediate threat. This principle ensures that your actions match the danger you're facing, and using defensive measures was a sensible thing to do given the situation.

The idea of necessity finds a balance between your right to protect yourself or others and the need to make sure your response is suitable and justified. Assessing necessity involves looking at factors like how urgent the threat is, if there were other options available, and whether the level of force used makes sense for the situation.

The principle of necessity in self-defence within legal rules helps prevent the use of too much force and decides if defensive actions taken against perceived threats are lawful.

When someone says they acted in self-defence, showing they honestly believed using force was necessary is crucial. This ensures that their response was based on a real evaluation of the danger, not influenced by other motives. This criterion stops people from making up reasons for aggressive actions and emphasises that self-defence should come from a genuine fear of immediate harm.

For a belief to be considered "honest," it usually means the person genuinely thought there was a threat and acted based on that perception, regardless of whether they were ultimately right. The law often cares more about the sincerity of the belief than how accurate the threat was, as long as the belief was reasonable given the circumstances.

In legal assessments of self-defence claims, an honest belief in the necessity of force is crucial. This ensures that people aren't punished for acting in what they genuinely believed was a life-threatening situation.

THE USE OF DEFENSIVE FORCE DEEMED REASONABLE GIVEN THE CIRCUMSTANCES

Using defensive force that's considered reasonable means that any actions taken to protect yourself must be fitting and in proportion to the immediate danger you're facing. In legal terms, this principle ensures that the level of force used isn't too much or unjustified, but rather matches the threat you're dealing with.

When looking at self-defence claims, the idea of reasonableness involves considering things like how serious the threat is, what other options were available, and how much force was needed to eliminate the danger. The response should be measured to get rid of the threat without going overboard.

The principle of reasonableness is crucial to stop the use of excessive force. It prevents people from using self-defence as an excuse for actions that go beyond what's necessary for personal safety or protecting others. The law usually expects individuals to show restraint and choose the least harmful way to counteract the threat.

Deciding if defensive force was reasonable is a crucial factor in determining if someone's actions in self-defence are legal.

It ensures that the response matches the immediate danger and follows the legal rules for using force in those situations.

The Criminal Justice and Immigration Act 2008, Section 76, introduces rules about using force in self-defence and preventing crime. This section focuses on using force to stop a crime or help in a lawful arrest. It says that the use of force must be seen as reasonable and proportionate based on the circumstances. The section also emphasises that judging reasonableness should consider how the person saw the threat, how much force was used, and the nature of the situation. Section 76 aims to balance the right of individuals to protect themselves or others with the need to make sure force is not more than necessary. It lines up with broader legal principles about self-defence and using force appropriately in different situations.

HOUSEHOLDER CASES

"Householder cases" in the Criminal Justice and Immigration Act 2008 refer to situations where homeowners use force to defend themselves, others, or their property within their own home. This term is used to distinguish cases where people are defending their homes from situations where they are not.

Section 76 of the Act specifically talks about using force in self-defence and preventing crime in householder cases. It sets out the rules and principles for the legality of using force in these situations. The section highlights that individuals have the right to protect themselves, others, and prevent crime using reasonable and proportionate force within their own homes.

In householder cases, the law understands the unique dynamics of defending one's home. The usual principles of reasonableness, proportionality, and necessity still apply, but the law considers the understandable instinct of homeowners to protect their property and loved ones from threats.

In non-householder cases, the same principles of reasonableness, proportionality, and necessity apply. Individuals who are not homeowners still have the right to use reasonable and proportionate force to protect themselves, others, and prevent crime from immediate threats.

Distinguishing between householder and non-householder cases helps deal with different situations and gives a legal structure for deciding if using force is lawful or not.

DEFENDANT CHARACTERISTICS AND THE PERCEPTION OF DANGER

Defendant characteristics and the perception of danger play a significant role in legal considerations. These factors influence how an individual's actions are evaluated in cases where defensive force is employed. Here's how they interplay:

Defendant Characteristics: This includes personal things about the person, like how old they are, their physical and mental health, and their past experiences. These factors influence how they see and react to a threat. Courts look at these characteristics to decide if their actions were reasonable based on their specific situation.

Perception of Danger: It's all about how the person facing danger sees the threat. If they genuinely thought they or others were in immediate danger, their actions might be considered justified. The law cares about what the person believed, checking if their perception of danger was honest and sensible in that situation.

How a person's personal traits and how they see danger interact highlights the importance of looking closely at the details in self-defence cases. It understands that people might see situations differently based on who they are and what they've been through. The law tries to find a balance between individual rights and keeping society safe. It recognises that responses to threats can differ but insists on using force reasonably and appropriately.

THE DUTY TO RETREAT

While there's no strict rule saying you must retreat in self-defence situations, the context matters. If there's a reasonable chance to step back and using force isn't necessary, it might affect whether your self-defence claim holds up. But remember, you're not forced to retreat, and it can still be okay to stand your ground if other self-defence conditions are met.

Common law focuses on broader self-defence principles, considering how immediate the threat is, whether you genuinely believe force is necessary, and if your actions make sense. Not having a strict duty to retreat gives people more flexibility in how they respond to threats, as long as their actions are justifiable under the law.

THE IMMINENCE OF THE THREATENED ATTACK

The "imminence of the threatened attack" is crucial in deciding if self-defence actions are legal in law. It's about how close and urgent the threat of harm is when defensive actions are taken. Legally, it checks if the danger is so immediate that there's a real and urgent need to respond.

In self-defence cases, the law usually says the threat must be imminent for defensive force to be okay. This means the danger has to be right there, happening now, giving the person little or no time to choose another way before using protective measures. Figuring out imminence looks at things like how close the threat is, what's happening, and the potential harm.

If someone reasonably believes they're facing an immediate threat and their actions match the danger, their use of force might be allowed under self-defence. The idea of imminence is important to make sure people don't use too much force against threats that aren't really happening right away.

Ultimately, the consideration of the imminence of the threatened attack ensures that self-defence claims are rooted in genuine and immediate perceptions of danger, rather than being used as a pretext for unwarranted aggression.

EXCESSIVE SELF-DEFENCE

Excessive self-defence, or using too much force, happens when someone goes beyond what's reasonably needed to protect themselves, others, or their property from an immediate threat. Legally, it's considered excessive when the level of force used is too much compared to the danger.

The law insists on proportionality in self-defence, meaning the defensive actions should match the threat. Using more force than necessary might lead to a self-defence claim being seen as unjustified.

In cases of excessive self-defence, the law tries to find a balance between an individual's right to protect themselves and the need to avoid unnecessary and potentially harmful force. If it's decided that the force used was too much for the situation, there could be legal consequences, from criminal charges to civil liabilities.

To decide if self-defence was excessive, factors like the type of threat, other options available, and the person's belief in the need for force are considered.

Courts check if a reasonable person, facing the same situation, would have reacted similarly. Following the idea of proportionality, the legal system ensures that self-defence stays within reasonable and justifiable limits.

In Australia, there used to be a historical approach where courts saw excessive self-defence as a partial excuse. If someone used too much force resulting in a death, they might be charged with manslaughter instead of murder. This recognised that while the response was too much, it didn't fully warrant a murder charge because excessive self-defence partially lessened the person's blame.

But this approach is no longer the norm in Australia. Courts don't see excessive self-defence as a separate thing leading to reduced charges. Instead, they look at each case's specific details to decide the right charges and potential defences.

It's essential to note that in English law, the House of Lords confirmed that excessive self-defence as a partial excuse is not officially recognised.

THE LEGISLATION

The law on self defence arises both under the common law defence of self-defence and the defences provided by section 3(1) of the Criminal Law Act 1967 (use of force in the prevention of crime or making arrest). Section 76 of the Criminal Justice and Immigration Act 2008 provides clarification of the operation of the existing common law and statutory defences.

Criminal Law Act 1967 s.3

3 Use of force in making arrest, etc.

(1) A person may use such force as is reasonable in the circumstances in the prevention of crime, or in effecting or assisting in the lawful arrest of offenders or suspected offenders or of persons unlawfully at large.

(2) Subsection (1) above shall replace the rules of the common law on the question when force used for a purpose mentioned in the subsection is justified by that purpose.

Both Section 3 and the common law principles concerning defensive force must be interpreted within the context of the Criminal Justice and Immigration Act 2008 Section 76.

Criminal Justice and Immigration Act 2008 Section 76.

76 Reasonable force for purposes of self-defence etc.

(1)This section applies where in proceedings for an offence—

(a)an issue arises as to whether a person charged with the offence ("D") is entitled to rely on a defence within subsection (2), and

(b)the question arises whether the degree of force used by D against a person ("V") was reasonable in the circumstances.

(2)The defences are—

(a)the common law defence of self-defence;

(aa)the common law defence of defence of property; and

(b)the defences provided by section 3(1) of the Criminal Law Act 1967 (c. 58) or section 3(1) of the Criminal Law Act (Northern Ireland) 1967 (c. 18 (N.I.)) (use of force in prevention of crime or making arrest).

(3)The question whether the degree of force used by D was reasonable in the circumstances is to be decided by reference to the circumstances as D believed them to be, and subsections (4) to (8) also apply in connection with deciding that question.

(4)If D claims to have held a particular belief as regards the existence of any circumstances—

(a)the reasonableness or otherwise of that belief is relevant to the question whether D genuinely held it; but

(b)if it is determined that D did genuinely hold it, D is entitled to rely on it for the purposes of subsection (3), whether or not—

(i)it was mistaken, or

(ii)(if it was mistaken) the mistake was a reasonable one to have made.

(5)But subsection (4)(b) does not enable D to rely on any mistaken belief attributable to intoxication that was voluntarily induced.

(5A)In a householder case, the degree of force used by D is not to be regarded as having been reasonable in the circumstances as D believed them to be if it was grossly disproportionate in those circumstances.

(6)In a case other than a householder case, the degree of force used by D is not to be regarded as having been reasonable in the circumstances as D believed them to be if it was disproportionate in those circumstances.

(6A)In deciding the question mentioned in subsection (3), a possibility that D could have retreated is to be considered (so far as relevant) as a factor to be taken into account, rather than as giving rise to a duty to retreat.

(7)In deciding the question mentioned in subsection (3) the following considerations are to be taken into account (so far as relevant in the circumstances of the case)—

(a)that a person acting for a legitimate purpose may not be able to weigh to a nicety the exact measure of any necessary action; and

(b)that evidence of a person's having only done what the person honestly and instinctively thought was necessary for a legitimate purpose constitutes strong evidence that only reasonable action was taken by that person for that purpose.

(8)Subsections (6A) and (7) are not to be read as preventing other matters from being taken into account where they are relevant to deciding the question mentioned in subsection (3).

(8A)For the purposes of this section "a householder case" is a case where—

(a)the defence concerned is the common law defence of self-defence,

(b)the force concerned is force used by D while in or partly in a building, or part of a building, that is a dwelling or is forces accommodation (or is both),

(c)D is not a trespasser at the time the force is used, and

(d)at that time D believed V to be in, or entering, the building or part as a trespasser.

(8B)Where—

(a)a part of a building is a dwelling where D dwells,

(b)another part of the building is a place of work for D or another person who dwells in the first part, and

(c)that other part is internally accessible from the first part, that other part, and any internal means of access between the two parts, are each treated for the purposes of subsection (8A) as a part of a building that is a dwelling.

(8C)Where—

 (a)a part of a building is forces accommodation that is living or sleeping accommodation for D,

 (b)another part of the building is a place of work for D or another person for whom the first part is living or sleeping accommodation, and

 (c)that other part is internally accessible from the first part, that other part, and any internal means of access between the two parts, are each treated for the purposes of subsection (8A) as a part of a building that is forces accommodation.

(8D)Subsections (4) and (5) apply for the purposes of subsection (8A)(d) as they apply for the purposes of subsection (3).

(8E)The fact that a person derives title from a trespasser, or has the permission of a trespasser, does not prevent the person from being a trespasser for the purposes of subsection (8A).

(8F)In subsections (8A) to (8C)—

  "building" includes a vehicle or vessel, and

  "forces accommodation" means service living accommodation for the purposes of Part 3 of the Armed Forces Act 2006 by virtue of section 96(1) (a) or (b) of that Act.

(9)This section, except so far as making different provision for householder cases, is intended to clarify the operation of the existing defences mentioned in subsection (2).

(10)In this section—

 (a)"legitimate purpose" means—

 (i)the purpose of self-defence under the common law,

 (ia)the purpose of defence of property under the common law, or

 (ii)the prevention of crime or effecting or assisting in the lawful arrest of persons mentioned in the provisions referred to in subsection (2)(b);

 (b)references to self-defence include acting in defence of another person; and

 (c)references to the degree of force used are to the type and amount of force used.

CONCLUSION

Self-defence is a basic part of criminal law that deals with a person's right to protect themselves or others from immediate harm. Legal judgments about self-defense consider factors like the need for defensive action, a sincere belief in using force, and whether the response was reasonable.

English law focuses on necessity, reasonableness, and proportionality when assessing self-defence. While there's no strict duty to retreat, how urgent the threat is and the situation matter. The legal system aims to balance individual rights and public safety, looking at both the person defending themselves and how they see the danger.

Avoiding excessive self-defence is crucial. The law doesn't want people using too much force in response to threats.

Understanding self-defence requires looking closely at each situation to decide if the actions were legal and justified. The changes in legal views show an ongoing effort to balance personal rights and public safety, making sure defensive actions follow the law.

CASES:

PALMER V R, [1971] AC 814

LEGISLATION

CRIMINAL JUSTICE AND IMMIGRATION ACT 2008 SECTION 76.

CRIMINAL LAW ACT 1967 S.3

THE EUROPEAN CONVENTION ON HUMAN RIGHTS (1950). ARTICLE 2.

NOTES

While this book falls within the legal genre, it serves purely informational purposes. It should not be construed as legal advice.

www.ingramcontent.com/pod-product-compliance
Lightning Source LLC
Chambersburg PA
CBHW060020300526
45794CB00003B/1227